Obama, Mandela & Doctor King Jn

Inspirational Quotes to Inspire the World Today

PROF LOBIANE FRANCIS RAKOTSOANE

ISBN: 1475205732

ISBN 13:   9781475205732

Library of Congress Control Number: 2012907981
CreateSpace, North Charleston, SC

Table of Contents

Introduction

The world has seen many great leaders whose contribution to humanity's welfare has inspired people across racial lines, generational gaps and international boundaries. However, in recent times, there has hardly been anyone with such highly inspirational leadership as Barack Obama, Nelson Mandela and Martin Luther King Jr. The quest of these three for global peace and prosperity for all as well as their identification with the rights of the poor and the marginalized of the world has earned them admirers the world over. The Nobel Peace Prize presented to each of them indicates just how much admiration they have enjoyed globally.

Their common message of hope in a world that is dominated by fear and despair has given— and continues to give— millions of those who suffer from all sorts of injustices a powerful inspiration and motivation that nothing is impossible where there is a will to succeed. No leader of African descent has captured the world's attention and given its people hope for a better future than these three. Their pithy and vivid quotes presented in this book are meant to inspire not only young and upcoming leaders, but everyone who reads this book so that a dream of a better world for all— a dream so well and eloquently articulated in these three men's speeches— may finally be realized.

Inspired by King's speech, "I have a dream", both Obama and Mandela have managed to achieve what many considered almost impossible. They have defied great odds to become the first black presidents of their nations and have remained an inspiration (each in his own right) despite the many unfounded racist attacks by their critics. It is my hope that in a world so full of depressing experiences, a book like this will lead to the emergence of other great leaders in our communities. Imagine how different our world would be with more Obamas, Mandelas and Kings!

1

Barack Obama

"The Norwegian Nobel committee has decided that the Nobel Peace Prize for 2009 is to be awarded to President Barack Obama for his extraordinary efforts to strengthen international diplomacy and cooperation between peoples. The committee has attached special importance to Obama's vision of and work for a world without nuclear weapons.

Obama has, as president of the United States, created a new climate in international politics. Multilateral diplomacy has regained a central position, with emphasis on the role that the United Nations and other international institutions can play. Dialogue and negotiations are preferred as instruments for resolving even the most difficult international conflicts. The vision of a world free from nuclear arms has powerfully stimulated disarmament and arms control negotiations. Thanks to Obama's initiative, the USA is now playing a more constructive role in meeting the great climatic challenges the world is confronting. Democracy and human rights are to be strengthened.

Only very rarely has a person to the same extent as Obama captured the world's attention and given its people hope for a better future. His diplomacy is founded in the concept that those who are to lead the world must do so on the basis of values and attitudes that are shared by the majority of the world's population.

For 108 years, the Norwegian Nobel committee has sought to stimulate precisely that international policy and those attitudes for which Obama is now the world's leading spokesman. The committee endorses Obama's appeal that 'Now is the time for all of us to take our share of responsibility for a global response to global challenges'."

(http://www.guardian.co.uk/world/2009/oct/09/nobel-peace-prize-citation-obama.)

2

Barack Obama Quotes

I am convinced that in order to move forward, we must say openly to each other the things we hold in our hearts and that too often are said only behind closed doors. There must be a sustained effort to listen to each other; to learn from each other; to respect one another.

When people are judged by merit, not connections, then the best and brightest can lead the country, people will work hard, and the entire economy will grow — everyone will benefit and more resources will be available for all, not just select groups.

When you serve, it doesn't just improve your community; it makes you a part of your community. It breaks down walls. It fosters cooperation.

All of us have a responsibility to work for the day when the mothers of Israelis and Palestinians can see their children grow up without fear; when the holy land of the three great faiths is the place of peace that God intended it to be; when Jerusalem is a secure and lasting home for Jews and Christians and Muslims and a place for all of the children of Abraham to mingle peacefully together as in the story of Isra, when Moses, Jesus, and Mohammed — peace be upon them — joined in prayer.

All of us share this world for but a brief moment in time. The question is whether we spend that time focused on what pushes us apart or whether we commit ourselves to an effort, a sustained effort to find common ground, to focus on the future we seek for our children and to respect the dignity of all human beings.

Making our economy work means making sure it works for everybody; that there are no second-class citizens in our workplaces.

If we think that we can secure our country by just talking tough without acting tough and smart, then we will misunderstand this moment and miss its opportunities. If we think that we can use the same partisan playbook where we just challenge our opponent's patriotism to win an election, then the American people will lose. The times are too serious for this kind of politics.

For we know that our patchwork heritage is a strength, not a weakness. We are a nation of Christians and Muslims, Jews and Hindus, and non-believers. We are shaped by every language and culture, drawn from every end of this Earth; and because we have tasted the bitter swill of civil war and segregation, and emerged from that dark chapter stronger and more united, we cannot help but believe that the old hatreds shall someday pass; that the lines of tribe shall soon dissolve; that as the world grows smaller, our common humanity shall reveal itself; and that America must play its role in ushering in a new era of peace.

I will never forget that the only reason I'm standing here today is because somebody, somewhere stood up for me when it was risky. Stood up when it was hard. Stood up when it wasn't popular. And because that somebody stood up, a few more stood up. And then a few thousand stood up. And then a few million stood up. And standing up, with courage and clear purpose, they somehow managed to change the world.

Secularists are wrong when they ask believers to leave their religion at the door before entering into the public square. Frederick Douglas, Abraham Lincoln, Williams Jennings Bryant, Dorothy Day, Martin Luther King — indeed, the majority of great reformers in American history — were not only motivated by faith, but repeatedly used religious language to argue for their cause.

To the Muslim world, we seek a new way forward, based on mutual interest and mutual respect. To those leaders around the globe who seek to sow conflict, or blame their society's ills on the West — know that your people will judge you on what you can build, not what you destroy. To those who cling to power through corruption and deceit and the silencing of dissent, know that you are on the wrong side of history; but that we will extend a hand if you are willing to unclench your fist.

I think that one of the things that we all agree to is that the touchstone for economic policy is, does it allow the average American to find good employment and see their incomes rise; that we can't just look at things in the aggregate — we do want to grow the pie, but we want to make sure that prosperity is spread across the spectrum of regions and occupations and genders and races; and that economic policy should focus on growing the pie, but it also has to make sure that everybody has got opportunity in that system.

Change doesn't come *from* Washington. Change comes *to* Washington.

Civil society is the conscience of our communities, and America will always extend our engagement abroad with citizens.

The strongest foundation for human progress lies in open economies, open societies, and open governments.

Experience shows us that history is on the side of liberty.

Those of us who are friends of Israel must understand that true security for the Jewish state requires an independent Palestine.

Nine years ago, the destruction of the World Trade Center signaled a threat that respected no boundary of dignity or decency.

We know this is no ordinary time for our people. Each of us comes here with our own problems and priorities.

The obligation of government is to empower the people, not impede them.

Israel's existence must not be subject for debate.

The slaughter of innocent Israelis is not resistance — it's injustice.

If you're walking down the right path and you're willing to keep walking, eventually you'll make progress.

Whenever I write a letter to a family who has lost a loved one in Iraq, or read an e-mail from a constituent who has dropped out of college because her student aid has been cut, I'm reminded that the actions of those in power have enormous consequences — a price that they themselves almost never have to pay.

Iraq is sort of a situation where you've got a guy who drove the bus into the ditch. You obviously have to get the bus out of the ditch, and that's not easy to do, although you probably should fire the driver.

My faith reminds me that we all are sinners.

Making your mark on the world is hard. If it were easy, everybody would do it. But it's not. It takes patience, it takes commitment, and it comes with plenty of failure along the way. The real test is not whether you avoid this failure, because you won't. It's whether you let it harden or shame you into inaction, or whether you learn from it; whether you choose to persevere.

When we send our young men and women into harm's way, we have a solemn obligation not to fudge the numbers or shade the truth about why they're going, to care for their families while they're gone, to tend to the soldiers upon their return, and to never, ever go to war without enough troops to win the war, secure the peace, and earn the respect of the world.

I have seen the desperation and disorder of the powerless —how it twists the lives of children on the streets of Jakarta or Nairobi in much the same way as it does the lives of children on Chicago's South Side.

We should be more modest in our belief that we can impose democracy on a country through military force. In the past, it has been movements for freedom from within tyrannical regimes that have led to flourishing democracies.

We lose ourselves when we compromise the very ideals that we fight to defend. And we honor those ideals by upholding them not when it's easy, but when it is hard.

This notion that's peddled by the religious right — that they are oppressed — is not true. Sometimes it's a cynical ploy to move their agenda ahead. The classic example being that somehow secularists are trying to eliminate Christmas, which strikes me as some kind of manufactured controversy.

The strongest democracies flourish from frequent and lively debate, but they endure when people of every background and belief find a way to set aside smaller differences in service of a greater purpose.

Running for the presidency is a profound decision — a decision no one should make on the basis of media hype or personal ambition alone. And so before I committed myself and my family to this race, I wanted to be sure that it was right for us and more importantly right for the country.

When I was growing up, basically the only black men on television were criminals or Flip Wilson dressed in drag as a character called Geraldine. But you rarely had black professionals portrayed in the culture.

I stand here knowing that my story is part of the larger American story, that I owe a debt to all of those who came before me, and that in no other country on Earth is my story even possible.

I don't oppose all wars. What I am opposed to is a dumb war. What I am opposed to is a rash war.

A good compromise, a good piece of legislation, is like a good sentence or a good piece of music. Everybody can recognize it. They say, 'Huh. It works. It makes sense.'

Three months is a lifetime in politics.

In the end, that's what this election is about. Do we participate in a politics of cynicism, or do we participate in a politics of hope?

I believe in evolution, scientific inquiry, and global warming; I believe in free speech, whether politically correct or politically incorrect and I am suspicious of using government to impose anybody's religious beliefs — including my own — on nonbelievers.

While we breathe, we will hope.

My little girls can break my heart. They can make me cry just looking at them eating their string beans.

It's only when you hitch your wagon to something larger than yourself that you realize your true potential.

If we aren't willing to pay a price for our values, then we should ask ourselves whether we truly believe in them at all.

I've got two daughters: 9 years old and 6 years old. I am going to teach them first of all about values and morals. But if they make a mistake, I don't want them punished with a baby.

I am not in favor of concealed weapons. I think that creates a potential atmosphere where more innocent people could get shot during altercations.

We have proved that the true strength of our nation comes not from the scale of our wealth but from the power of our ideals: opportunity, democracy, liberty and hope.

Instead of having a set of policies that are equipping people for the globalization of the economy, we have policies that are accelerating the most destructive trends of the global economy.

Money is not the only answer, but it makes a difference.

That my father looked nothing like the people around me — that he was black as pitch, my mother white as milk — barely registered in my mind.

My parents shared not only an improbable love; they shared an abiding faith in the possibilities of this nation. They would give me an African name, Barack, or blessed, believing that in a tolerant America your name is no barrier to success. They imagined me going to the best schools in the land, even though they weren't rich, because in a generous America you don't have to be rich to achieve your potential.

I didn't run for president so that the dreams of our daughters could be deferred or denied. I didn't run for president to see inequality and injustice persist in our time.

We live in a culture that discourages empathy. A culture that too often tells us our principal goal in life is to be rich, thin, young, famous, safe, and entertained.

You know, my faith is one that admits some doubt.

This is the moment when we must come together to save this planet. Let us resolve that we will not leave our children a world where the oceans rise and famine spreads and terrible storms devastate our lands.

There are patriots who opposed the war in Iraq and there are patriots who supported the war in Iraq. We are one people, all of us pledging allegiance to the stars and stripes, all of us defending the United States of America.

I recognize there is a certain presumptuousness in this, a certain audacity, to this announcement. I know that I haven't spent a lot of time learning the ways of Washington, but I've been there long enough to know that the ways of Washington must change. People who love their country can change it.

It took a lot of blood, sweat, and tears to get to where we are today, but we have just begun. Today we begin in earnest the work of making sure that the world we leave our children is just a little bit better than the one we inhabit today.

My job is not to represent Washington to you, but to represent you to Washington.

Tonight, we gather to affirm the greatness of our nation — not because of the height of our skyscrapers, or the power of our military, or the size of our economy. Our pride is based on a very simple premise, summed up in a declaration made over two hundred years ago.

Where the stakes are the highest in the war on terror, we cannot possibly succeed without extraordinary international cooperation. Effective international police actions require the highest degree of intelligence sharing, planning, and collaborative enforcement.

Community colleges play an important role in helping people transition between careers by providing the retooling they need to take on a new career.

With the changing economy, no one has lifetime employment. But community colleges provide lifetime employability.

We have an obligation and a responsibility to be investing in our students and our schools. We must make sure that people who have the grades, the desire, and the will, but not the money, can still get the best education possible.

We need to steer clear of this poverty of ambition, where people want to drive fancy cars and wear nice clothes and live in nice apartments but don't want to work hard to accomplish these things. Everyone should try to realize their full potential.

All across the world, in every kind of environment and region known to man, increasingly dangerous weather patterns and devastating storms are abruptly putting an end to the long-running debate over whether or not climate change is real. Not only is it real, it's here, and its effects are giving rise to a frighteningly new global phenomenon: the man-made natural disaster.

Today we're seeing that climate change is about more than a few unseasonably mild winters or hot summers. It's about the chain of natural catastrophes and devastating weather patterns that global warming is beginning to set off around the world — the frequency and intensity of which are breaking records thousands of years old.

The issue of climate change is one that we ignore at our own peril. There may still be disputes about exactly how much we're contributing to the warming of the earth's atmosphere and how much is naturally occurring, but what we can be scientifically certain of is that our continued use of fossil fuels is pushing us to a point of no return. And unless we free ourselves from a dependence on these fossil fuels and chart a new course on energy in this country, we are condemning future generations to global catastrophe.

In my heart I know you didn't come here just for me; you came here because you believe in what this country can be. In the face of war, you believe there can be peace. In the face of despair, you believe there can be hope. In the face of a politics that's shut you out, that's told you to settle, that's divided us for too long, you believe we can be one people, reaching for what's possible, building that more perfect union.

That is the true genius of America: a faith in the simple dreams of its people, the insistence on small miracles. That we can say what we think, write what we think, without hearing a sudden knock on the door; that we can have an idea and start our own business without paying a bribe or hearing a sudden knock on the door. That we can participate in the political process without fear of retribution, and that our votes will be counted — or at least, most of the time.

People don't expect government to solve all their problems. But they sense, deep in their bones, that with just a slight change in priorities, we can make sure that every child in America has a decent shot at life, and that the doors of opportunity remain open to all. They know we can do better.

I stand here today as hopeful as ever that the United States of America will endure, that it will prevail, that the dream of our founders will live on in our time.

To ensure prosperity here at home and peace abroad, we all share the belief we have to maintain the strongest military on the planet.

If there is anyone out there who still doubts that America is a place where all things are possible; who still wonders if the dream of our founders is alive in our time; who still questions the power of our democracy, tonight is your answer.

To those Americans whose support I have yet to earn: I may not have won your vote, but I hear your voices, I need your help, and I will be your president, too.

We've got a tragic history when it comes to race in this country. We've got a lot of pent-up anger and bitterness and misunderstanding — This country wants to move beyond these kinds of things.

But the anger is real; it is powerful; and to simply wish it away, to condemn it without understanding its roots, only serves to widen the chasm of misunderstanding that exists between the races.

We have been told we cannot do this by a chorus of cynics who will only grow louder and more dissonant in the weeks to come. We've been asked to pause for a reality check. We've been warned against offering the people of this nation false hope. But in the unlikely story that is America, there has never been anything false about hope. For when we have faced down impossible odds, when we've been told that we're not ready, or that we shouldn't try, or that we can't, generations of Americans have responded with a simple creed that sums up the spirit of a people: Yes, we can.

If I sit down with the leader of Iran, I will send him a strong message that Israel is our friend, that we will assist in their security and that we don't find nuclear weapons acceptable — That's not going to be a propaganda coup for the president of Iran.

I'm in this race not just to hold an office, but to gather with you to transform a nation.

This campaign can't only be about me — It must be about what we can do together.

In the face of impossible odds, people who love their country can change it.

We're not going to baby-sit a civil war.

Do we participate in a politics of cynicism or a politics of hope?

Let us recognize what unites us across borders and build on the strength of this blessed country. Let us embrace our history and our legacy.

This is our time and I'm grateful to be a part of that.

After a century of striving, after a year of debate, after a historic vote, health care reform is no longer an unmet promise. It is the law of the land.

Al-Qaeda is still a threat. We cannot pretend somehow that because Barack Hussein Obama got elected as president, suddenly everything is going to be OK.

Americans still believe in an America where anything's possible — they just don't think their leaders do.

And I will do everything that I can as long as I am President of the United States to remind the American people that we are one nation under God, and we may call that God different names but we remain one nation.

As I've said, there were patriots who supported this war, and patriots who opposed it. And all of us are united in appreciation for our servicemen and women, and our hopes for (the) Iraqis' future.

Change will not come if we wait for some other person or some other time. We are the ones we've been waiting for. We are the change that we seek.

Contrary to the claims of some of my critics and some of the editorial pages, I am an ardent believer in the free market.

I consider it part of my responsibility as president of the United States to fight against negative stereotypes of Islam wherever they appear.

I don't care whether you're driving a hybrid or an SUV. If you're headed for a cliff, you have to change direction. That's what the American people called for in November, and that's what we intend to deliver.

I know my country has not perfected itself. At times, we've struggled to keep the promise of liberty and equality for all of our people. We've made our share of mistakes, and there are times when our actions around the world have not lived up to our best intentions.

I think it is important for Europe to understand that even though I am president and George Bush is not president, Al-Qaeda is still a threat.

I think when you spread the wealth around, it's good for everybody.

If the people cannot trust their government to do the job for which it exists — to protect them and to promote their common welfare — all else is lost.

In America, there's a failure to appreciate Europe's leading role in the world.

Issues are never simple. One thing I'm proud of is that very rarely will you hear me simplify the issues.

It was not a religion that attacked us that September day. It was al-Qaeda. We will not sacrifice the liberties we cherish or hunker down behind walls of suspicion and mistrust.

It's time to fundamentally change the way that we do business in Washington. To help build a new foundation for the twenty-first century, we need to reform our government so that it is more efficient, more transparent, and more creative. That will demand new thinking and a new sense of responsibility for every dollar that is spent.

Now, anybody who thinks that we can move this economy forward with just a few folks at the top doing well, hoping that it's going to trickle down to working people who are running faster and faster just to keep up, you'll never see it.

Of course, violence will not end with our combat mission. Extremists will continue to set off bombs, attack Iraqi civilians, and try to spark sectarian strife. But ultimately, these terrorists will fail to achieve their goals.

One of the great strengths of the United States is we have a very large Christian population — we do not consider ourselves a Christian nation or a Jewish nation or a Muslim nation. We consider ourselves a nation of citizens who are bound by ideals and a set of values.

Operations in Iraq and Afghanistan and the war on terrorism have reduced the pace of military transformation and have revealed our lack of preparation for defensive and stability operations. This Administration has overextended our military.

Our combat mission is ending, but our commitment to Iraq's future is not.

People of Berlin — people of the world — this is our moment. This is our time.

Poorly secured nuclear material in the former Soviet Union, or secrets from a scientist in Pakistan, could help build a bomb that detonates in Paris. The poppies in Afghanistan become the heroin in Berlin. The poverty and violence in Somalia breeds the terror of tomorrow.

Since I'm the president and Democrats have controlled the House and the Senate, it's understandable that people are saying, you know, 'What have you done?'

So while an incredible amount of progress has been made, on this fifth anniversary, I wanted to come here and tell the people of this city directly: My administration is going to stand with you — and fight alongside you — until the job is done. Until New Orleans is all the way back, all the way.

The Bush Administration's failure to be consistently involved in helping Israel achieve peace with the Palestinians has been both wrong for our friendship with Israel, as well as badly damaging to our standing in the Arab world.

The fact that my fifteen minutes of fame has extended a little longer than fifteen minutes is somewhat surprising to me and completely baffling to my wife.

The thing about hip-hop today is it's smart; it's insightful. The way they can communicate a complex message in a very short space is remarkable.

The United States has been enriched by Muslim Americans. Many other Americans have Muslims in their families or have lived in a Muslim-majority country — I know, because I am one of them.

The United States is not, and never will be, at war with Islam.

Today we are engaged in a deadly global struggle for those who would intimidate, torture, and murder people for exercising the most basic freedoms. If we are to win this struggle and spread those freedoms, we must keep our own moral compass pointed in a true direction.

We all knew this. We all knew that it would take more time than any of us want to dig ourselves out of this hole created by this economic crisis.

We cannot continue to rely only on our military in order to achieve the national security objectives that we've set. We've got to have a civilian national security force that's just as powerful, just as strong, just as well-funded.

We didn't become the most prosperous country in the world just by rewarding greed and recklessness. We didn't come this far by letting the special interests run wild. We didn't do it just by gambling and chasing paper profits on Wall Street. We built this country by making things, by producing goods we could sell.

We have real enemies in the world. These enemies must be found. They must be pursued and they must be defeated.

We need somebody who's got the heart, the empathy, to recognize what it's like to be a young teenage mom, the empathy to understand what it's like to be poor or African-American or gay or disabled or old — and that's the criterion by which I'll be selecting my judges.

We need to internalize this idea of excellence. Not many folks spend a lot of time trying to be excellent.

We've persevered because of a belief we share with the Iraqi people — a belief that out of the ashes of war, a new beginning could be born in this cradle of civilization. Through this remarkable chapter in the history of the United States and Iraq, we have met our responsibility. Now, it's time to turn the page.

What I worry about would be that you essentially have two chambers, the House and the Senate, but you have simply, majoritarian, absolute power on either side. And that's just not what the founders intended.

What Washington needs is adult supervision.

When we think of the major threats to our national security, the first to come to mind are nuclear proliferation, rogue states and global terrorism. But another kind of threat lurks beyond our shores, one from nature, not humans — an avian flu pandemic.

The best way to not feel hopeless is to get up and do something. Don't wait for good things to happen to you. If you go out and make some good things happen, you will fill the world with hope; you will fill yourself with hope.

A change is brought about because ordinary people do extraordinary things.

We are the change we have been waiting for.

In the unlikely story that is America, there has never been anything false about hope.

If there's a child on the south side of Chicago who can't read, that matters to me, even if it's not my child. If there's a senior citizen somewhere who can't pay for their prescription, who has to choose between medicine and the rent, that makes my life poorer — even if it's not my grandparent. If there's an Arab American or Mexican American family being rounded up by John Ashcroft without benefit of an attorney or due process, I know that that threatens my civil liberties. And I don't have to be a woman to be concerned that the Supreme Court is trying to take away a woman's right, because I know that my rights are next. It is that fundamental belief — I am my brother's keeper, I am my sister's keeper — that makes this country work.

We don't ask you to believe in our ability to bring change; rather, we ask you to believe in yours.

Nothing can stand in the way of the power of millions of voices calling for change.

I'm inspired by the people I meet in my travels — hearing their stories, seeing the hardships they overcome, their fundamental optimism and decency. I'm inspired by the love people have for their children. And I'm inspired by my own children, how full they make my heart. They make me want to work to make the world a little bit better. And they make me want to be a better man.

One voice can change a room, and if one voice can change a room, then it can change a city, and if it can change a city, it can change a state, and if it change a state, it can change a nation, and if it can change a nation, it can change the world. Your voice can change the world.

What I've realized is that life doesn't count for much unless you're willing to do your small part to leave our children — all of our children — a better world. Any fool can have a child. That doesn't make you a father. It's the courage to raise a child that makes you a father.

More than a building that houses books and data, the library has always been a window to a larger world — a place where we've always come to discover big ideas and profound concepts that help move the American story forward.

Libraries remind us that truth isn't about who yells the loudest, but who has the right information. Because even as we're the most religious of people, America's innovative genius has always been preserved because we also have a deep faith in facts.

And so the moment we persuade a child, any child, to cross that threshold into a library, we've changed their lives forever, and for the better. This is an enormous force for good.

Our challenges may be new. The instruments with which we meet them may be new. But those values upon which our success depends — honesty and hard work, courage and fair play, tolerance and curiosity, loyalty and patriotism — these things are old. These things are true. They have been the quiet force of progress throughout our history. What is demanded then is a return to these truths. What is required of us now is a new era of responsibility — a recognition, on the part of every American, that we have duties to ourselves, our nation, and the world, duties that we do not grudgingly accept but rather seize gladly, firm in the knowledge that there is nothing so satisfying to the spirit, so defining of our character, than giving our all to a difficult task.

The American story has never been about things coming easy: It has been about rising to the moment when the moment is hard; about rejecting panicked division for purposeful unity; about seeing a mountaintop from the deepest valley. That is why we remember that some of the most famous words ever spoken by an American came from a president who took office in a time of turmoil: "The only thing we have to fear is fear itself."

Here's the truth: the Soviet Union had thousands of nuclear weapons, and Iran doesn't have a single one. But when the world was on the brink of nuclear holocaust, Kennedy talked to Khrushchev and he got those missiles out of

Cuba. Why shouldn't we have the same courage and the confidence to talk to our enemies? That's what strong countries do; that's what strong presidents do; that's what I'll do when I'm president of the United States of America.

To all those watching tonight from beyond our shores, from parliaments and palaces, to those who are huddled around radios in the forgotten corners of the world, our stories are singular, but our destiny is shared, and a new dawn of American leadership is at hand.

All too rarely do I hear people asking just what it is that we've done to make so many children's hearts so hard, or what collectively we might do to right their moral compass — what values we must live by.

The true test of the American ideal is whether we're able to recognize our failings and then rise together to meet the challenges of our time. Whether we allow ourselves to be shaped by events and history, or whether we act to shape them. Whether chance of birth or circumstance decides life's big winners and losers, or whether we build a community where, at the very least, everyone has a chance to work hard, get ahead, and reach their dreams.

In an interconnected world, the defeat of international terrorism — and most importantly, the prevention of these terrorist organizations from obtaining weapons of mass destruction — will require the cooperation of many nations...

The strongest democracies flourish from frequent and lively debate, but they endure when people of every background and belief find a way to set aside smaller differences in service of a greater purpose.

America is a land of big dreamers and big hopes. It is this hope that has sustained us through revolution and civil war, depression and world war, a struggle for civil and social rights, and the brink of nuclear crisis. And it is because our dreamers dreamed that we have emerged from each challenge more united, more prosperous, and more admired than before.

The success of our economy has always depended not just on the size of our gross domestic product, but on the reach of our prosperity, on the ability to extend opportunity to every willing heart — not out of charity, but because it is the surest route to our common good.

In a global economy where the most valuable skill you can sell is your knowledge, a good education is no longer just a pathway to opportunity — it is a pre-requisite.

I always believe that ultimately, if people are paying attention, then we get good government and good leadership. And when we get lazy, as a democracy and civically start taking shortcuts, then it results in bad government and politics.

When special interests put their thumb on the scale, and distort the free market, the people who compete by the rules come in last.

I'm happy to get good ideas from across the political spectrum, from Democrats and Republicans. What I won't do is return to the failed theories of the last eight years that got us into this fix in the first place, because those theories have been tested, and they have failed.

The best judge of whether or not a country is going to develop is how it treats its women. If it's educating its girls, if women have equal rights, that country is going to move forward. But if women are oppressed and abused and illiterate, then they're going to fall behind.

With the magnitude of the challenges we face right now, what we need in Washington are not more political tactics — we need more good ideas. We don't need more point-scoring — we need more problem-solving.

The war does not end when you come home. It lives on in memories of your fellow soldiers, sailors, airmen and Marines who gave their lives. It endures in the wound that is slow to heal, the disability that isn't going away, the dream that wakes you at night, or the stiffening in your spine when a car backfires down the street.

One of the most durable and destructive legacies of discrimination is the way we've internalized a sense of limitation; how so many in our community have come to expect so little from the world and from themselves.

No system of government can or should be imposed upon one nation by any other. That does not lessen my commitment, however, to governments that reflect the will of the people. Each nation gives life to this principle in its own way, grounded in the traditions of its own people. America does not presume to know what is best for everyone, just as we would not presume to pick the outcome of a peaceful election. But I do have an unyielding belief that all people yearn for certain things: the ability to speak your mind and have a say in how you are governed; confidence in the rule of law and the equal administration of justice; government that is transparent and doesn't steal from the people; the freedom to live as you choose.

You can't let your failures define you — you have to let your failures teach you. You have to let them show you what to do differently the next time.

Focusing your life solely on making a buck shows a poverty of ambition. It asks too little of yourself. And it will leave you unfulfilled.

In a country of 300 million people, there is a certain degree of audacity required for anybody to say, "I'm the best person to lead this country."

Faith is not just something you have; it's something you do.

Race is still a powerful force in this country. Any African American candidate, or any Latino candidate, or Asian candidate or woman candidate, confronts a higher threshold in establishing himself to the voters ... Are some voters not going to vote for me because I'm African American? Those are the same voters who probably wouldn't vote for me because of my politics.

Our enemies are fully aware that they can use oil as a weapon against America. And if we don't take this threat as seriously as the bombs they build or the guns they buy, we will be fighting the War on Terror with one hand tied behind our back.

We should never forget that God granted us the power to reason so that we would do His work here on Earth — so that we would use science to cure disease, and heal the sick, and save lives.

Everybody knows politics is a contact sport.

People are very hungry for something new. I think they are interested in being called to be a part of something larger than the sort of small, petty, slash-and-burn politics that we have been seeing over the last several years.

We have come to be consumed by a 24-hour, slash-and-burn, negative ad, bickering, small-minded politics that doesn't move us forward. Sometimes one side is up and the other side is down. But there is no sense that they are coming together in a common-sense, practical, non-ideological way to solve the problems that we face.

We have a stake in one another ... what binds us together is greater than what drives us apart, and ... if enough people believe in the truth of that proposition and act on it, then we might not solve every problem, but we can get something meaningful done for the people with whom we share this Earth.

Our goal is to have a country that's not divided by race. And my impression, as I travel around the country, is that that's the kind of country that most people want, as well, and that we all have prejudice, we all have certain suspicions or stereotypes about people who are different from us, whether it's religious or racial or ethnic, but what I think I found in the American people, I think there's a core decency there, where if they take the time, if they get the time to know individuals, then they want to judge those individuals by their character.

We have to acknowledge the progress we made, but understand that we still have a long way to go; that things are better, but still not good enough.

We think of faith as a source of comfort and understanding but find our expression of faith sowing division; we believe ourselves to be a tolerant people even as racial, religious, and cultural tensions roil the landscape. And instead of resolving these tensions or mediating these conflicts, our politics fans them, exploits them, and drives us further apart.

I trust the American people to realize that while we don't need big government, we do need a government that stands up for families who are being tricked out of their homes by Wall Street predators; a government that stands up for the middle-class by giving them a tax break; a government that ensures that no American will ever lose their life savings just because their child gets sick. Security and opportunity; compassion and prosperity aren't liberal values or conservative values — they're American values.

We can't change the way Washington works unless we first change how Congress works.

Stereotypes and prejudices still exist in American society, and for the highest office in the land a female or African American candidate would, at the outset, confront some additional hurdles to show that they were qualified and competent. But what I've found is that the American people — once they get to know you — are going to judge you on your individual character. Whatever the flaws in the process, people get a fairly accurate read by the end of the campaign.

We must be as careful getting out of Iraq as we were careless getting in.

Most people who serve in Washington have been trained either as lawyers or as political operatives — professions that tend to place a premium on winning arguments rather than solving problems.

We've gotta restore the American people's confidence in the ethics process by ensuring that political self-interest can no longer prevent politicians from enforcing ethics rules.

Politics has become so bitter and partisan, so gummed up by money and influence, that we can't tackle the big problems that demand solutions. And that's what we have to change first. We have to change our politics, and come together around our common interests and concerns as Americans.

In the end, no amount of American forces can solve the political differences that lie at the heart of somebody else's civil war.

Of all the rocks upon which we build our lives, we are reminded today that family is the most important. And we are called to recognize and honor how critical every father is to that foundation. They are teachers and coaches. They are mentors and role models. They are examples of success and the men who constantly push us toward it. But if we are honest with ourselves, we'll admit that what too many fathers also are is missing — missing from too many lives and too many homes. They have abandoned their responsibilities, acting like boys instead of men. And the foundations of our families are weaker because of it.

I have asserted a firm conviction rooted in my faith in God and my faith in the American people — that working together we can move beyond some of our old racial wounds, and that in fact we have no choice if we are to continue on the path of a more perfect union.

If those Republicans come at me with the same fear-mongering and swift-boating that they usually do, then I will take them head on. Because I believe the American people are tired of fear and tired of distractions and tired of diversions. We can make this election not about fear, but about the future. And that won't just be a Democratic victory; that will be an American victory.

Life doesn't count for much unless you're willing to do your small part to leave our children — all of our children — a better world. Even if it's difficult. Even if the work seems great. Even if we don't get very far in our lifetime.

Our government should work for us, not against us. It should help us, not hurt us. It should ensure opportunity not just for those with the most money and influence, but for every American who's willing to work. That's the promise of America: the idea that we are responsible for ourselves, but that we also rise or fall as one nation; the fundamental belief that I am my brother's keeper; I am my sister's keeper.

We need not throw away 200 years of American jurisprudence while we fight terrorism. We need not choose between our most deeply held values, and keeping this nation safe.

You don't defeat a terrorist network that operates in eighty countries by occupying Iraq.

The government can't solve every problem, but an enlightened government can make sure that people can work hard for their dreams and achieve them.

When you start just focusing exclusively on trying to tear the other person down instead of what you are going to do on behalf of the American people to deal with this economy, then that's not serving Democrats, that's not serving Republicans, that's not serving anybody.

This country of ours has more wealth than any nation, but that's not what makes us rich. We have the most powerful military on Earth, but that's not what makes us strong. Our universities and our culture are the envy of the world, but that's not what keeps the world coming to our shores. Instead, it is that American spirit — that American promise — that pushes us forward even when the path is uncertain; that binds us together in spite of our differences; that makes us fix our eye not on what is seen, but what is unseen, that better place around the bend.

Part of America's genius has always been its ability to absorb newcomers, to forge a national identity out of the disparate lot that arrived on our shores.

So we have a choice to make. We can once again let Washington's bad habits stand in the way of progress. Or we can pull together and say that in America, our destiny isn't written for us, but by us. We can place good ideas ahead of old ideological battles, and a sense of purpose above the same narrow partisanship. We can act boldly to turn crisis into opportunity and, together, write the next great chapter in our history and meet the test of our time.

People have asked me, when did it hit you that you are now president? And what I told them was the most sobering moment is signing letters to the families of our fallen heroes. It reminds you of the responsibilities that you carry in this office and — the consequences of the decisions that you make.

To truly transform our economy, protect our security, and save our planet from the ravages of climate change, we need to ultimately make clean, renewable energy the profitable kind of energy.

There are some who question the scale of our ambitions, who suggest that our system cannot tolerate too many big plans. Their memories are short, for they have forgotten what this country has already done, what free men and women can achieve when imagination is joined to common purpose, and necessity to courage.

My whole goal over the next four years is to make sure that, whatever arguments are persuasive and backed up by evidence and facts and proof that they can work, that we are pulling people together around that kind of pragmatic agenda.

Nowhere is it ordained that history moves in a straight line.

Any strategy to reduce intergenerational poverty has to be centered on work, not welfare--not only because work provides independence and income but also because work provides order, structure, dignity, and opportunities for growth in people's lives.

I am the eternal optimist. I think that, over time, people respond to civility and rational argument.

The answers to our problems don't lie beyond our reach. They exist in our laboratories and universities; in our fields and our factories; in the imaginations of our entrepreneurs and the pride of the hardest-working people on Earth.

Those qualities that have made America the greatest force of progress and prosperity in human history we still possess in ample measure.

What Americans expect from Washington is action that matches the urgency they feel in their daily lives.

It is time to put in place tough, new, common-sense rules of the road so that our financial market rewards drive and innovation, and punishes short-cuts and abuse.

In a world that's more and more interconnected, we all have responsibilities to work together to solve common challenges.

I'm confident that at this defining moment, we will prove ourselves worthy of the sacrifice of those who came before us, and the promise of those who will come after.

You know, it's hard for twenty heads of state to bridge their differences. We've all got our own national policies; we all have our own assumptions, our own political cultures. But our citizens are all hurting. They all need us to come together.

The countries who out-educate us today will out-compete us tomorrow.

I've often said that I don't believe government has the answer to every problem or that it can do all things for all people. We are a nation built on the strength of individual initiative. But there are certain things that we can't do on our own. There are certain things only a government can do.

The consequences of war are dire, the sacrifices immeasurable. We may have occasion in our lifetime to once again rise up in defense of our freedom, and pay the wages of war. But we ought not—we will not—travel down that hellish path blindly.

At times, American foreign policy has been farsighted, simultaneously serving our national interests, our ideals, and the interests of other nations. At other times American policies have been misguided, based on false assumptions that ignore the legitimate aspirations of other peoples, undermine our own credibility, and make for a more dangerous world.

Ultimately, the challenges of the twenty-first century can't be met without collective action. Agreement will almost never be easy, and results won't always come quickly. But I am committed to respecting different points of view, and to forging a consensus instead of dictating our terms ... that's how we will advance and uphold our ideals.

We'll recover from this recession, but it will take time, it will take patience, and it will take an understanding that, when we all work together, when each of us looks beyond our own short-term interest to the wider set of obligations we have towards each other, that's when we succeed, that's when we prosper, and that's what is needed right now.

Hostility and hatred are no match for justice; they offer no pathway to peace.

If we neglect or abandon those who are suffering in poverty, not only are we depriving ourselves of potential opportunities for markets and economic growth, but ultimately that despair may turn to violence that turns on us.

Globalization makes our economy, our health, and our security all captive to events on the other side of the world. And no other nation on Earth has a greater capacity to shape that global system, or to build consensus around a new set of international rules that expand the zones of freedom, personal safety, and economic well-being. Like it or not, if we want to make America more secure, we are going to have to help make the world more secure.

We cannot meet the challenges of today with old habits and stale thinking. So much of our government was built to deal with different challenges from a different era. Too often, the result is wasteful spending, bloated programs, and inefficient results. It's time to fundamentally change the way that we do business in Washington. To help build a new foundation for the twenty-first century, we need to reform our government so that it is more efficient, more transparent, and more creative. That will demand new thinking and a new sense of responsibility for every dollar that is spent.

The Declaration of Independence, the Constitution, the Bill of Rights are not simply words written into aging parchment. They are the foundation of liberty and justice in this country, and a light that shines for all who seek freedom, fairness, equality and dignity in the world.

Many ... are simply skeptical that real change can occur. There is so much fear, so much mistrust that has built up over the years. But if we choose to be bound by the past, we will never move forward. And I want to particularly say this to young people of every faith in every country: You more than anyone have the ability to reimagine the world, to remake this world.

Suppressing ideas never succeeds in making them go away.

Part of my job, I think, is to bridge that gap between the status quo and what we know we have to do for our future.

So long as our relationship is defined by our differences, we will empower those who sow hatred rather than peace, those who promote conflict rather than the cooperation that can help all of our people achieve justice and prosperity. This cycle of suspicion and discord must end.

The interests we share as human beings are far more powerful than the forces that drive us apart.

I think the big challenge that we've got on education is making sure that from kindergarten or pre-kindergarten through your fourteenth or fifteenth year of school, or sixteenth year of school, or twentieth year of school, that you are actually learning the kinds of skills that make you competitive and productive in a modern, technological economy.

Whatever we think of the past, we must not be prisoners to it.

We must never alter or forget our principles. 9/11 was an enormous trauma to our country. The fear and anger that it provoked was understandable. But in some cases, it led us to act contrary to our traditions and our ideals.

Violence is a dead end. It is a sign neither of courage nor power to shoot rockets at sleeping children or to blow up old women on a bus. That's not how moral authority is claimed; that's how it is surrendered.

Discrimination cannot stand — not on account of color or gender; how you worship or who you love. Prejudice has no place in the United States of America.

We did not come to fear the future. We came here to shape it.

If we want this country to succeed in the twenty-first century, we've got to lay a new foundation for lasting prosperity.

Now as we begin to put an end to this recession, we have to consider what comes next — because we can't afford to return to an economy based on inflated profits and maxed-out credit cards; an economy where we depend on dirty and outdated sources of energy; an economy where we're burdened by soaring health care costs that serve only the special interests. This won't create sustainable growth, it won't shrink our deficit, and it won't create jobs.

I have no interest in putting insurance companies out of business. They provide a legitimate service, and employ a lot of our friends and neighbors. I just want to hold them accountable.

Every single one of you has something that you're good at. Every single one of you has something to offer. And you have a responsibility to yourself to discover what that is. That's the opportunity an education can provide.

Where you are right now doesn't have to determine where you'll end up. No one's written your destiny for you, because here in America, you write your own destiny. You make your own future.

Asking for help isn't a sign of weakness; it's a sign of strength because it shows you have the courage to admit when you don't know something, and that then allows you to learn something new.

When it comes to education, we got to get past this whole paradigm, this outdated notion that somehow it's just money, or somehow it's just reform, but no money, and embrace what Dr. King called the "both-and" philosophy. We need more money and we need more reform.

I've called Chicago home for nearly twenty-five years. It's a city of broad shoulders and big hearts and bold dreams; a city of legendary sports figures, legendary sports venues, and legendary sports fans; a city like America itself, where the world — the world's races and religions and nationalities come together and reach for the dream that brought them here.

It's important to realize that I was actually black before the election.

Although we may come from vastly different stories and very different walks of life, we are one people who possess common values and common ideals; who celebrate individual excellence but also share a recognition that together, we can accomplish great and wonderful things we can't accomplish alone.

3

Nelson Mandela

"Nelson Rolihlahla Mandela (born July 18, 1918) is a former president of South Africa, the first to be elected in fully representative democratic elections. Before his presidency, Mandela was an anti-apartheid activist and leader of the African National Congress (ANC) and its armed wing Umkhonto we Sizwe. He spent 27 years in prison, much of it in a cell on Robben Island, on convictions for crimes that included sabotage committed while he spearheaded the struggle against apartheid. Among opponents of apartheid in South Africa and internationally, he became a symbol of freedom and equality, while the apartheid government and nations sympathetic to it condemned him and the ANC as communists and terrorists. Following his release from prison in 1990, his switch to a policy of reconciliation and negotiation helped lead the transition to multi-racial democracy in South Africa. Since the end of apartheid, he has been widely praised, even by former opponents. Mandela has received more than one hundred awards over four decades, most notably the Nobel Peace Prize in 1993. He is currently a celebrated elder statesman who continues to voice his opinion on topical issues. In South Africa he is often known as Madiba, an honorary title adopted by elders of Mandela's clan. The title has come to be synonymous with Nelson Mandela."

(http://www.robertatchison.com/mandela/)

4

Nelson Mandela Quotes

During my lifetime I have dedicated myself to this struggle of the African people; I have fought against white domination; and I have fought against black domination. I have cherished the ideal of a democratic and free society in which all persons live together in harmony and with equal opportunities. It is an ideal which I hope to live for and to achieve. But if it needs be, it is an ideal for which I am prepared to die.

Let it never be said by future generations that indifference, cynicism, or selfishness made us fail to live up to the ideals of humanism which the Nobel Peace Prize encapsulates. Let the strivings of us all prove Martin Luther King Jr. to have been correct, when he said that humanity can no longer be tragically bound to the starless midnight of racism and war.

How can I be expected to believe that this same racial discrimination, which has been the cause of so much injustice and suffering right through the years, should now operate here to give me a fair and open trial?....I consider myself neither morally nor legally obliged to obey laws made by a Parliament in which I am not represented. That the will of the people is the basis of the authority of government, is a principle universally acknowledged as sacred throughout the civilized world.

Let there be justice for all. Let there be peace for all. Let there be work, bread, water and salt for all. Let each know that for each the body, the mind, and the soul have been freed to fulfill themselves.

I have never cared very much for personal prizes. A man does not become a freedom fighter in the hope of winning awards, but when I was notified that I had won the 1993 Nobel Peace Prize jointly with Mr. de Klerk, I was deeply moved. The Nobel Peace Prize had a special meaning to me because of its involvement with South African history.... The award was a tribute to all South Africans and especially to those who fought in the struggle; I would accept it on their behalf.

Friends, comrades and fellow South Africans: I greet you all in the name of peace, democracy, and freedom for all. I stand here before you not as a prophet but as a humble servant of you, the people. Your tireless and heroic sacrifices have made it possible for me to be here today. I therefore place the remaining years of my life in your hands.

Education is the great engine of personal development. It is through education that the daughter of a peasant can become a doctor, that a son of a mineworker can become the head of the mine, that a child of farm workers can become the president of a great nation. It is what we make out of what we have, not what we are given, that separates one person from another.

That was one of the things that worried me — to be raised to the position of a semi-god — because then you are no longer a human being. I wanted to be known as Mandela, a man with weaknesses, some of which are fundamental, and a man who is committed, but never-the-less, sometimes he fails to live up to expectations.

When I think about the past, the types of things they did, I feel angry, but then again that is my feeling. The brain always dominates, says, as I have pointed out, you have a limited time to stay on Earth. You must try and use that period to transform your country into what you desire it to be.

The curious beauty of African music is that it uplifts even as it tells a sad tale. You may be poor, you may have only a ramshackle house, you may have lost your job, but that song gives you hope. African music is often about the aspirations of the African people, and it can ignite the political resolve of those who might otherwise be indifferent to politics.

I have walked that long road to freedom. I have tried not to falter; I have made missteps along the way. But I have discovered the secret that after climbing a great hill, one only finds that there are many more hills to climb. I have taken a moment here to rest, to steal a view of the glorious vista that surrounds me, to look back on the distance I have come. But I can only rest for a moment, for with freedom comes responsibilities, and I dare not linger, for my long walk is not ended.

As a leader...I have always endeavored to listen to what each and every person in a discussion had to say before venturing my own opinion. Oftentimes, my own opinion will simply represent a consensus of what I heard in the discussion. I always remember the axiom: a leader...is like a shepherd. He stays behind the flock, letting the most nimble go out ahead, whereupon the others follow, not realizing that all along they are being directed from behind.

I regard it as a duty which I owed, not just to my people, but also to my profession, to the practice of law, and to the justice for all mankind, to cry out against this discrimination which is essentially unjust and opposed to the whole basis of the attitude towards justice which is part of the tradition of legal training in this country. I believed that in taking up a stand against this injustice I was upholding the dignity of what should be an honorable profession.

You can see that, there is no easy walk to freedom anywhere and many of us will have to pass through the valley of the shadow of death again and again before we reach the mountain tops of our desires. Dangers and difficulties have not deterred us in the past; they will not frighten us now. But we must be prepared for them, like men who mean business and who do not waste energy in vain talk and idle action. The way of preparation for action lies in our rooting out all impurity and indiscipline from our organization and making it the bright and shining instrument that will cleave its way to Africa's freedom.

The government has interpreted the peacefulness of the movement as a weakness: the people's non-violent policies have been taken as a green light for government violence. Refusal to resort to force has been interpreted by the government as an invitation to use armed force against the people without any fear of reprisals.

There was much in such a society that was primitive and insecure and it certainly could never measure up to the demands of the present epoch. But in such a society are contained the seeds of revolutionary democracy in which none will be held in slavery or servitude, and in which poverty, want, and insecurity shall be no more. This is the inspiration which, even today, inspires me and my colleagues in our political struggle.

It was the government that should have been told to refrain from its inhuman policy of violence and massacre, not the African people. It was further argued that it is wrong and indefensible for a political organization to repudiate picketing, which is used the world over as a legitimate form of pressure to prevent scabbing. Even up to the present day the question that is being asked with monotonous regularity up and down the country is this: Is it politically correct to continue preaching peace and non-violence when dealing with a government whose barbaric practices have brought so much suffering and misery to Africans?

It is, however, well known that the main national liberation organizations in this country have consistently followed a policy of non-violence. They have conducted themselves peaceably at all times, regardless of government attacks and persecutions upon them, and despite all government-inspired attempts to provoke them to violence. They have done so because the people prefer peaceful methods of change to achieve their aspirations without the suffering and bitterness of civil war.

There can be no keener revelation of a society's soul than the way in which it treats its children.

The time comes in the life of any nation when there remain only two choices — submit or fight. That time has now come to South Africa. We shall not submit and we have no choice but to hit back by all means in our power in defense of our people, our future, and our freedom.

Whatever the sentence Your Worship sees fit to impose upon me for the crime for which I have been convicted before this court, may it rest assured that when my sentence has been completed, I will still be moved as men are always moved, by their conscience. I will still be moved by my dislike of the race discrimination against my people. When I come out from serving my sentence, I will take up again, as best I can, the struggle for the removal of those injustices until they are finally abolished.

This is one of the most important moments in the life of our country. I stand here before you filled with deep pride and joy — pride in the ordinary, humble people of this country. You have shown such calm, patient determination to reclaim this country as your own, and now the joy that we can loudly proclaim from the rooftops — Free at last! Free at last! I stand before you humbled by your courage, with a heart full of love for you. I regard it as the highest honor to lead the ANC at this moment in our history. I am your servant. It is not the individuals that matter, but the collective. This is the time to heal the old wounds and build a new South Africa.

Of all the observations I have made on the strike, none has brought forth so much heat and emotion as the stress and emphasis we put on non-violence. Our most loyal supporters, whose courage and devotion has never been doubted, unanimously and strenuously disagreed with this approach and with the assurances we gave that we would not use any form of intimidation whatsoever to induce people to stay away from work. It was argued that the soil of our beloved country has been stained with the priceless blood of African patriots murdered by the Nationalist government in the course of peaceful and disciplined demonstrations to assert their claims and legitimate aspirations.

I cherish my own freedom dearly, but I care even more for your freedom. Too many have died since I went to prison. Too many have suffered for the love of freedom. I owe it to their widows, to their orphans, to their mothers and their fathers, who have grieved and wept for them ... Not only have I suffered during these long, lonely, wasted years. I am no less life-loving than you are. But I cannot sell the birthright of the people to be free ... Only free men can negotiate. Prisoners cannot enter into contracts. Your freedom and mine cannot be separated.

I hate racial discrimination most intensely and all its manifestations. I have fought all my life; I fight now, and will do so until the end of my days. Even although I now happen to be tried by one whose opinion I hold in high esteem, I detest most violently the set-up that surrounds me here. It makes me feel that I am a black man in a white man's court. This should not be I should feel perfectly at ease and at home with the assurance that I am being tried by a fellow South African, who does not regard me as an inferior, entitled to a special type of justice.

Today the majority of South Africans, black and white, recognize that apartheid has no future. It has to be ended by our own decisive mass action in order to build peace and security. The mass campaign of defiance and other actions of our organization and people can only culminate with the establishment of democracy... The factors which necessitated the armed struggle still exist today. We have no option but to continue. We express the hope that a climate conducive to a negotiated settlement will be created soon so that there may no longer be the need for the armed struggle.

I cannot conceive of Israel withdrawing if Arab states do not recognize Israel, within secure borders.

As we are liberated from our own fear, our presence automatically liberates others.

As I have said, the first thing is to be honest with yourself. You can never have an impact on society if you have not changed yourself... Great peacemakers are all people of integrity, of honesty, but humility.

I dream of the realization of the unity of Africa, whereby its leaders combine in their efforts to solve the problems of this continent. I dream of our vast deserts, of our forests, of all our great wildernesses.

I learned that courage was not the absence of fear, but the triumph over it. The brave man is not he who does not feel afraid, but he who conquers that fear.

A good head and a good heart are always a formidable combination.

Communists have always played an active role in the fight by colonial countries for their freedom, because the short-term objects of communism would always correspond with the long-term objects of freedom movements.

Does anybody really think that they didn't get what they had because they didn't have the talent or the strength or the endurance or the commitment?

Education is the most powerful weapon which you can use to change the world.

For to be free is not merely to cast off one's chains, but to live in a way that respects and enhances the freedom of others.

I detest racialism, because I regard it as a barbaric thing, whether it comes from a black man or a white man.

I dream of an Africa which is in peace with itself.

If there are dreams about a beautiful South Africa, there are also roads that lead to their goal. Two of these roads could be named Goodness and Forgiveness.

If you talk to a man in a language he understands, that goes to his head. If you talk to him in his language, that goes to his heart.

If you want to make peace with your enemy, you have to work with your enemy. Then he becomes your partner.

In my country we go to prison first and then become president.

It always seems impossible until it is done.

It is better to lead from behind and to put others in front, especially when you celebrate victory when nice things occur. You take the front line when there is danger. Then people will appreciate your leadership.

Let freedom reign. The sun never set on so glorious a human achievement.

Money won't create success; the freedom to make it will.

Never, never, and never again shall it be that this beautiful land will again experience the oppression of one by another.

There is no easy walk to freedom anywhere, and many of us will have to pass through the valley of the shadow of death again and again before we reach the mountaintop of our desires.

There is no passion to be found playing small - in settling for a life that is less than the one you are capable of living.

There is no such thing as "part freedom."

We must use time wisely and forever realize that the time is always ripe to do right.

When the water starts boiling, it is foolish to turn off the heat.

I am not a saint, unless you think of a saint as a sinner who keeps on trying.

Sometimes it falls upon a generation to be great. You can be that great generation.

Like slavery and apartheid, poverty is not natural. It is man-made and it can be overcome and eradicated by the actions of human beings.

No one is born hating another person because of the color of his skin, or his background, or his religion. People must learn to hate, and if they can learn to hate, they can be taught to love, for love comes more naturally to the human heart than its opposite.

[A] new society cannot be created by reproducing the repugnant past, however refined or enticingly repackaged.

I was called a terrorist yesterday, but when I came out of jail, many people embraced me, including my enemies, and that is what I normally tell other people who say those who are struggling for liberation in their country are terrorists. I tell them that I was also a terrorist yesterday, but today I am admired by the very people who said I was one.

Freedom would be meaningless without security in the home and in the streets.

The greatest glory in living lies not in never falling, but in rising every time we fall.

Man's goodness is a flame that can be hidden but never extinguished.

A man who takes away another man's freedom is a prisoner of hatred; he is locked behind the bars of prejudice and narrow-mindedness. I am not truly free if I am taking away someone else's freedom, just as surely as I am not free when my freedom is taken from me. The oppressed and the oppressor alike are robbed of their humanity.

I really wanted to retire and rest and spend more time with my children, my grandchildren, and of course with my wife. But the problems are such that for anybody with a conscience who can use whatever influence he may have to try to bring about peace, it's difficult to say no.

Democracy is based on the majority principle. This is especially true in a country such as ours where the vast majority have been systematically denied their rights. At the same time, democracy also requires that the rights of political and other minorities be safeguarded.

When you let your own light shine, you unconsciously give others permission to do the same.

5

Martin Luther King, Jr.

"Martin Luther King, Jr. (January 15, 1929 — April 4, 1968) was an American clergyman, activist, and prominent leader in the African American civil rights movement. He is best known for being an iconic figure in the advancement of civil rights in the United States and around the world, using nonviolent methods following the teachings of Mahatma Gandhi. King is often presented as a heroic leader in the history of modern American liberalism.

A Baptist minister, King became a civil rights activist early in his career. He led the 1955 Montgomery Bus Boycott and helped found the Southern Christian Leadership Conference in 1957, serving as its first president. King's efforts led to the 1963 March on Washington, where King delivered his "I Have a Dream" speech. There, he expanded American values to include the vision of a color-blind society, and established his reputation as one of the greatest orators in American history.

In 1964, King became the youngest person to receive the Nobel Peace Prize for his work to end racial segregation and racial discrimination through civil disobedience and other nonviolent means. By the time of his death in 1968, he had refocused his efforts on ending poverty and stopping the Vietnam War.

King was assassinated on April 4, 1968, in Memphis, Tennessee. He was posthumously awarded the Presidential Medal of Freedom in 1977 and Congressional Gold Medal in 2004; Martin Luther King, Jr. Day was established as a U.S. national holiday in 1986."

(http://en.wikipedia.org/wiki/Martin_Luther_King,_Jr)

6

Martin Luther King, Jr. Quotes

I have a dream that my four little children will one day live in a nation where they will not be judged by the color of their skin, but by the content of their character.

I have a dream that one day every valley shall be exalted, every hill and mountain shall be made low, the rough places will be made straight, and the glory of the Lord shall be revealed and all flesh shall see it together.

I have a dream that one day on the red hills of Georgia, the sons of former slaves and the sons of former slave owners will be able to sit together at the table of brotherhood.

I just want to do God's will. And he's allowed me to go to the mountain. And I've looked over, and I've seen the Promised Land! I may not get there with you, but I want you to know tonight that we as a people will get to the Promised Land.

I refuse to accept the view that mankind is so tragically bound to the starless midnight of racism and war that the bright daybreak of peace and brotherhood can never become a reality... I believe that unarmed truth and unconditional love will have the final word.

We must develop and maintain the capacity to forgive. He who is devoid of the power to forgive is devoid of the power to love. There is some good in the worst of us and some evil in the best of us. When we discover this, we are less prone to hate our enemies.

We must learn to live together as brothers, or perish together as fools.

An individual has not started living until he can rise above the narrow confines of his individualistic concerns to the broader concerns of all humanity.

Change does not roll in on the wheels of inevitability, but comes through continuous struggle. And so we must straighten our backs and work for our freedom. A man can't ride you unless your back is bent.

Darkness cannot drive out darkness; only light can do that. Hate cannot drive out hate; only love can do that.

Human progress is neither automatic nor inevitable... Every step toward the goal of justice requires sacrifice, suffering, and struggle; the tireless exertions and passionate concern of dedicated individuals.

Whatever affects one directly, affects all indirectly. I can never be what I ought to be until you are what you ought to be. This is the interrelated structure of reality.

A genuine leader is not a searcher for consensus but a molder of consensus.

A lie cannot live.

A man who won't die for something is not fit to live.

A nation or civilization that continues to produce soft-minded men purchases its own spiritual death on the installment plan.

A nation that continues year after year to spend more money on military defense than on programs of social uplift is approaching spiritual doom.

A right delayed is a right denied.

A riot is the language of the unheard.

All labor that uplifts humanity has dignity and importance and should be undertaken with painstaking excellence.

All progress is precarious, and the solution of one problem brings us face to face with another problem.

Almost always, the creative, dedicated minority has made the world better.

An individual who breaks a law that conscience tells him is unjust, and who willingly accepts the penalty of imprisonment in order to arouse the conscience of the community over its injustice, is in reality expressing the highest respect for the law.

At the center of non-violence stands the principle of love.

Discrimination is a hellhound that gnaws at Negroes in every waking moment of their lives to remind them that the lie of their inferiority is accepted as truth in the society dominating them.

Every man must decide whether he will walk in the light of creative altruism or in the darkness of destructive selfishness.

Everything that we see is a shadow cast by that which we do not see.

Faith is taking the first step even when you don't see the whole staircase.

Freedom is never voluntarily given by the oppressor; it must be demanded by the oppressed.

Have we not come to such an impasse in the modern world that we must love our enemies - or else? The chain reaction of evil - hate begetting hate, wars producing more wars - must be broken, or else we shall be plunged into the dark abyss of annihilation.

He who passively accepts evil is as much involved in it as he who helps to perpetrate it. He who accepts evil without protesting against it is really cooperating with it.

History will have to record that the greatest tragedy of this period of social transition was not the strident clamor of the bad people, but the appalling silence of the good people.

Human salvation lies in the hands of the creatively maladjusted.

I am not interested in power for power's sake, but I'm interested in power that is moral, that is right, and that is good.

I believe that unarmed truth and unconditional love will have the final word in reality. This is why right, temporarily defeated, is stronger than evil, triumphant.

I have decided to stick with love. Hate is too great a burden to bear.

I look to a day when people will not be judged by the color of their skin, but by the content of their character.

I submit to you that if a man hasn't discovered something that he will die for, he isn't fit to live.

I want to be the white man's brother, not his brother-in-law.

If physical death is the price that I must pay to free my white brothers and sisters from a permanent death of the spirit, then nothing can be more redemptive.

If we are to go forward, we must go back and rediscover those precious values - that all reality hinges on moral foundations and that all reality has spiritual control.

In the end, we will remember not the words of our enemies, but the silence of our friends.

Injustice anywhere is a threat to justice everywhere.

It is incontestable and deplorable that Negroes have committed crimes, but they are derivative crimes. They are born of the greater crimes of the white society.

It is not enough to say we must not wage war. It is necessary to love peace and sacrifice for it.

It may be true that the law cannot make a man love me, but it can keep him from lynching me, and I think that's pretty important.

Law and order exist for the purpose of establishing justice and when they fail in this purpose, they become the dangerously structured dams that block the flow of social progress.

Life's most urgent question is: What are you doing for others?

Love is the only force capable of transforming an enemy into friend.

Means we use must be as pure as the ends we seek.

Never forget that everything Hitler did in Germany was legal.

Never succumb to the temptation of bitterness.

Nonviolence is a powerful and just weapon which cuts without wounding and ennobles the man who wields it. It is a sword that heals.

Nonviolence means avoiding not only external physical violence but also internal violence of spirit. You not only refuse to shoot a man, but you refuse to hate him.

Nothing in all the world is more dangerous than sincere ignorance and conscientious stupidity.

One of the greatest casualties of the war in Vietnam is the Great Society shot down on the battlefield of Vietnam.

Our lives begin to end the day we become silent about things that matter.

Our scientific power has outrun our spiritual power. We have guided missiles and misguided men.

Peace is not merely a distant goal that we seek, but a means by which we arrive at that goal.

Philanthropy is commendable, but it must not cause the philanthropist to overlook the circumstances of economic injustice which make philanthropy necessary.

Pity may represent little more than the impersonal concern which prompts the mailing of a check, but true sympathy is the personal concern which demands the giving of one's soul.

Property is intended to serve life, and no matter how much we surround it with rights and respect, it has no personal being. It is part of the earth man walks on. It is not man.

Rarely do we find men who willingly engage in hard, solid thinking. There is an almost universal quest for easy answers and half-baked solutions. Nothing pains some people more than having to think.

Science investigates; religion interprets. Science gives man knowledge, which is power; religion gives man wisdom, which is control.

Seeing is not always believing.

Shallow understanding from people of good-will is more frustrating than absolute misunderstanding from people of ill will.

Take the first step in faith. You don't have to see the whole staircase, just take the first step.

That old law about 'an eye for an eye' leaves everybody blind. The time is always right to do the right thing.

The art of acceptance is the art of making someone who has just done you a small favor wish that he might have done you a greater one.

The first question which the priest and the Levite asked was: "If I stop to help this man, what will happen to me?" But... the Good Samaritan reversed the question: "If I do not stop to help this man, what will happen to him?"

The function of education is to teach one to think intensively and to think critically. Intelligence plus character - that is the goal of true education.

The hope of a secure and livable world lies with disciplined nonconformists who are dedicated to justice, peace, and brotherhood.

The hottest place in Hell is reserved for those who remain neutral in times of great moral conflict.

The limitation of riots, moral questions aside, is that they cannot win and their participants know it. Hence, rioting is not revolutionary but reactionary because it invites defeat. It involves an emotional catharsis, but it must be followed by a sense of futility.

The moral arc of the universe bends at the elbow of justice.

The Negro needs the white man to free him from his fears. The white man needs the Negro to free him from his guilt.

The past is prophetic in that it asserts loudly that wars are poor chisels for carving out peaceful tomorrows.

The quality, not the longevity, of one's life is what is important.

The question is not whether we will be extremists, but what kind of extremists we will be... The nation and the world are in dire need of creative extremists.

The sweltering summer of the Negro's legitimate discontent will not pass until there is an invigorating autumn of freedom and equality.

The time is always right to do what is right.

The ultimate measure of a man is not where he stands in moments of comfort and convenience, but where he stands at times of challenge and controversy.

The ultimate tragedy is not the oppression and cruelty by the bad people, but the silence over that by the good people.

There can be no deep disappointment where there is not deep love.

There is nothing more tragic than to find an individual bogged down in the length of life, devoid of breadth.

To be a Christian without prayer is no more possible than to be alive without breathing.

War is a poor chisel to carve out tomorrow.

We are not makers of history. We are made by history.

We may have all come on different ships, but we're in the same boat now.

We must accept finite disappointment, but never lose infinite hope.

We must build dikes of courage to hold back the flood of fear.

We must concentrate not merely on the negative expulsion of war, but the positive affirmation of peace.

We must use time creatively.

We who in engage in nonviolent direct action are not the creators of tension. We merely bring to the surface the hidden tension that is already alive.

We will have to repent in this generation not merely for the vitriolic words and actions of the bad people, but for the appalling silence of the good people.

We will remember not the words of our enemies, but the silence of our friends.

Whatever your life's work is, do it well. A man should do his job so well that the living, the dead, and the unborn could do it no better.

When you are right you cannot be too radical; when you are wrong, you cannot be too conservative.

Nonviolence is the answer to the crucial political and moral questions of our time; the need for mankind to overcome oppression and violence without resorting to oppression and violence. Mankind must evolve for all human conflict a method which rejects revenge, aggression, and retaliation. The foundation of such a method is love.

Our loyalties must transcend our race, our tribe, our class, and our nation; and this means we must develop a world perspective.

A good many observers have remarked that if equality could come at once the Negro would not be ready for it. I submit that the white American is even more unprepared.

A man who won't die for something is not fit to live.

Hatred paralyses life; love releases it. Hatred confuses life; love harmonizes it. Hatred darkens life; love illuminates it.

Everybody can be great because anybody can serve. You don't have to have a college degree to serve. You don't have to make your subject and verb agree to serve. You only need a heart full of grace. A soul generated by love.

The Negro will only be truly free when he reaches down to the inner depths of his own being and signs with the pen and ink of assertive selfhood his own emancipation proclamation.

The ultimate solution to the race problem lies in the willingness of men to obey the unenforceable.

Psychological freedom, a firm sense of self-esteem, is the most powerful weapon against the long night of physical slavery.

We must combine the toughness of the serpent with the softness of the dove, a tough mind and a tender heart.

When evil men plot, good men must plan. When evil men burn and bomb, good men must build and bind. When evil men shout ugly words of hatred, good men must commit themselves to the glories of love.

Let us all hope that the dark clouds of racial prejudice will soon pass away, and that in some not-too-distant tomorrow the radiant stars of love and brotherhood will shine over our great nation with all their scintillating beauty.

If you succumb to the temptation of using violence in the struggle, unborn generations will be the recipients of a long and desolate night of bitterness, and your chief legacy to the future will be an endless reign of meaningless chaos.

In no sense do I advocate evading or defying the law. That would lead to anarchy.

Justice denied anywhere diminishes justice everywhere.

Yes, if you want to say that I was a drum major, say that I was a drum major for justice; say that I was a drum major for peace; I was a drum major for righteousness. I want to leave a committed life behind.

Man was born into barbarism when killing his fellow man was a normal condition of existence. He became endowed with a conscience. And he has now reached the day when violence toward another human being must become as abhorrent as eating another's flesh.

Morality cannot be legislated but behavior can be regulated. Judicial decrees may not change the heart, but they can restrain the heartless.

Non-violent action, the Negro saw, was the way to supplement, not replace, the progress of change. It was the way to divest himself of passivity with arraying himself in vindictive force.

Bibliography

http://www.guardian.co.uk/world/2009/oct/09/nobel-peace-prize-citation-obama.

http://www.thinkexist.com/english/Author/x/Author_3763_1.htm.

http://www.thinkexist.com/english/Author/x/Author_1793_1.htm.

http://www.notable-quotes.com/o/obama_barack.html

http://www.brainyquote.com/quotes/authors/n/nelson_mandela.html

http://www.saidwhat.co.uk/quotes/political/nelson_mandela

http://www.quotationspage.com/quotes/Nelson_Mandela/

http://www.notable-quotes.com/m/mandela_nelson.html

http://www.woopidoo.com/business_quotes/authors/nelson-mandela/index.htm

http://en.wikipedia.org/wiki/Martin_Luther_King,_Jr

http://www.brainyquote.com/quotes/authors/m/martin_luther_king_jr.html.

http://www.brainyquote.com/quotes/authors/b/barack_obama.html.

http://www.goodreads.com/author/quotes/6356.Barack_Obama.

http://www.squidoo.com/barack-obama-quotes-t-shirts.

http://www.allgreatquotes.com/barack_obama_quotes.shtml.

http://www.woopidoo.com/business_quotes/authors/barack-obama/index.htm.

http://www.mahalo.com/barack-obama-quotes.

http://www.finestquotes.com/author_quotes-author-Barack%20Obama-page-0.htm.

http://www.buzzle.com/articles/barack-obama-quotes.html.

http://www.greatpersonalities.com/barack-obama/.

The Editors of Essence. 2009. *The Obamas in the White House: Reflections on Family, Faith & Leadership.* New York: Time Inc. Home Entertainment